GW01319524

SWEET TORTURE
OF BREATHING

To Sarah

SWEET TORTURE
OF BREATHING
Lorna Thorpe

lots of love

Lorna xxx
Nov 2011

Arc
PUBLICATIONS
2011

Published by Arc Publications
Nanholme Mill, Shaw Wood Road
Todmorden OL14 6DA, UK
www.arcpublications.co.uk

Design by Tony Ward
Printed in Great Britain by the
MPG Book Group, Bodmin and King's Lynn

978 1906570 80 4 pbk
978 1906570 81 1 hbk

ACKNOWLEDGEMENTS
The author is grateful to the editors of the following
publications in which some of these poems, or ver-
sions of these poems, first appeared: *city lighthouse
poetry anthology* (Tall Lighthouse, 2009), *Envoi, Frogmore
Papers, Ink Sweat and Tears, Poetry South* (Pighog Press
and The South, 2007), *Poetry South East 2010* (The
Frogmore Press) and *Warwick Review.*

The author wishes to thank Hugh Dunkerley, Linda
France, Naomi Foyle, Martine Large, Kai Merriot,
Bethan Roberts, David Swann and Jackie Wills for
their criticism, advice and support.
    She would also like to thank Arts Council England
for a grant which assisted in the completion of this
book.

Cover image: 'Fashion model underwater in dolphin
tank, Marineland, Florida' by Toni Frissell, October 1939.
Reproduced by courtesy of the Library of Congress,
Toni Frissell Collection.

Supported by
ARTS COUNCIL
ENGLAND

Editor for the UK and Ireland: John W. Clarke

for Boris

Contents

PART 3

... Since then I have taken a lot of Prozac, Paxil, Welbutrin, Effexor, Ritalin, Focalin. I've also studied deeply in the philosophies and the religions, but cheerfulness kept breaking through.
LEONARD COHEN

Humankind cannot bear very much reality.
T. S. ELIOT

PART 1

This is your life

Once my life was buying hot rolls from the Jewish baker
in Waterloo Street at three in the morning; waking
to find the bed on fire because the candles I'd lit
before crashing into a coma had toppled over; dancing
on the tables of the Café de Paris on Sunday afternoons;
bricking it en route to the Spanish-French border
after flushing Chillum Dave's private stash down the loo,
the petrol tank of his Volvo packed with 25 kilos of hash.
There must have been dull moments, too, bill-paying,
phone calls to utility companies but I don't remember
anything like this tsunami of papers, I don't remember
ring-fencing an oasis of time in which to read
or watch an episode of *Six Feet Under*, worrying
I should be doing something else. I don't remember
worry at all and even guilt only showed up
at the appropriate times, when I copped off with a guy
my friend fancied or slipped a pair of hot pants
into my bag in the changing room of Peter Robinson's.
These days I'm as good as bloody gold but I'm forever
glancing over my shoulder in the Nothing to Declare lane,
counting minutes like Silas Marner, hoping for more
moments like the night my lover slid his hand
beneath the silk of my dress, rolled my stockings
to my ankles, told me to raise my leg and place my foot
on the chair, a moment that was so *Cabaret* I swear I heard
Joel Gray whispering: *Here even the orchestra is beautiful.*

Project Lorna

You take your injured bird of a psyche
to a series of therapists, hoping they will help you fly.

One sits in a room that smells of peaches, another
– a Jungian – has paintings of shadows on the wall.

You go thinking it's a problem of aerodynamics,
too much drag, too little lift in the air around you.

You're hoping to build a stairway to heaven,
a place where you'll never need the box of tissues

always so close to hand but they get you digging
instead, squinting into pokey corners, opening doors

to basements that could be enchanting, if they didn't insist
on sweeping out all the masks and cobwebby dreams,

switching on that fluorescent beam. But now you're hooked,
craving your fifty minute fix each week, hungry as a junkie

for your silver bullet. The question is, how will you know
when you've succeeded? Will you be a better person

or a more authentic one? Will you be more, or less,
angry, more or less, controlled? Will you be

fluent in all the dialects of psychotherapy, or will
the trick that saved you as a child – the one where you

chameleon yourself to the climate – be the death of you,
create a tower of Babel in your supermarket sweep of a mind?

In other words, how will you know whether this project will be the making or the breaking of me, me, me?

Lorna of the crows

I was also born
in a crow's nest in a valley
at the edge of Friston Forest
and on those nights
when I'm not at home
in my skin I shed it,
slick back my black feathers
and make for the graveyard
where I perch on a headstone –
I like the worn ones best, the ones
where the lettering has been eaten
away by wind, rain and time –
and bathe in the moonlight,
tapping my lizard-skin boots
and banging my head
to the party's-end smooch
of insects, the bone-snapping
tangos of the dead.

Distressing a mirror

They must see it all, those mute confidantes:
the junior assistant flicking ash from his chest
while his boss pulls on her trousers, failing
to disguise her haste; the middle-aged woman
on her second honeymoon, tetchily removing
basque, stockings, Russian Red lipstick
while her husband snores; the naked couple
admiring the action as he takes her from behind;
the salesman jerking off to *Greased and Oiled*
on pay-per-view; suitcases snapped open to reveal
stacks of notes, packs of heroin, hash, cocaine;
and now and then, a knife, a smoking gun,
a body bleeding into the mattress that last night
hosted a drunken threesome from Bulgaria.
Naturally, they all get their fair share of nose-picking,
nasal hair trimming, blackhead squeezing;
rehearsed speeches declaring love, confessing betrayal;
splatterings of water, toothpaste, cum.
I no longer have the mirror in front of which I died
and was resurrected but it must have been a treat,
a respite from the routine, that daytime soap opera
fading out into a scene from ER, complete
with defib paddles and a hot paramedic in Aviator shades.

Interlude

Six and a half minutes –
as long as you dare, long enough
for ice creams, a swift G&T at the bar,
a crafty fag outside. Chance
to analyse the first act, praise
the performance, slate the script,
wonder if the director had a clue
what she was doing, chance
to nip to the bathroom
before the curtain goes up
on the second act, in which
the leading lady is praying
for a set of new lines
along with the blood of strangers
and an all-singing, all-dancing heart.

Live in the moment

Book in one hand, spoon in the other,
the radio on in the background,
I read while stirring chicken risotto.
Outside, a dog barks and the confluence
of the steam from the pan, the smell
of wine and stock, the faint strains
of an aria live from the Met,
the poem I've just read, takes me back
to Christmas 1989, a cottage in the Wye Valley.
It's Boxing Day and I'm curled up with
Elizabeth David's *An Omelette and a Glass of Wine*,
while my lover – now dead – makes a casserole
with leftover turkey. When we hear the dogs
we step outside
to see the shooting party returning,
several brace of pheasants strung
from a fence. It's a cold day,
a light mist hanging over the fields.
Back at the stove I'm baptised
in the past, the smell of wood smoke
and turkey, the pine cones I'd gathered
on Christmas Eve and piled in bowls,
the holly, a shiver of something ancient
in the mistletoe hanging in the doorway,
the hounds baying in the mist.

*

I'm in a white room
with seven strangers, each of us
chewing a raisin, mindfully

19

noting taste, texture. We're learning
mindfulness, this season's feel-good,
manage-your-emotions tool, learning
to observe the comings and goings of our minds,
the wheeling and dealing, ducking and diving
as it's happening, without tainting the moment
with interfering concepts, labels, judgements
or ideas. Like all raisins, my raisin
is dry and wrinkled as a crone. My raisin is me.

*

Now imagine the moment itself, as shy
as a girl in a party frock, blinking and twitching
with each blinding flash of the camera
so part of her face is always in shadow.
Ask yourself why the moments in the books
and manuals are always red wheelbarrows,
soft rain on windows, freshly baked cookies
and the smell of newly mown grass. Ask yourself,
if all feelings, all moments, are meant to be equal,
where are the moments of pinched fury, of praying
for a downpour the day your neighbour
(who plays the drums and keeps you up all night
with his grooves and ghost strokes)
is having a barbeque? Where are the trashed poems,
the loneliness that travels through the arm
that hurls the egg against the wall; where the fragments
of shell, embedded in the paint for years?

Little pricks

Needless to say, I don't remember
every little prick

just the sensation of being
punctured:

some barely scratched
the surface

others provoked a twang
of shock

as of poking a live wire into
spleen, liver, heart.

Some days I felt the heady
rush of *qi*

but mostly I staggered away
dazed, unable

to scribble my name
or buckle my shoes.

Some say it started when soldiers
wounded by arrows

in battle were healed of ancient
afflictions,

others claim channels and meridians
are about as real

as lines of longitude and medieval
bodily humours.

I don't know about that but often,
as I lay there,

I'd picture myself sticking pins
in a voodoo doll

as needled as a pin cushion.

Mind, body and spirit

In the literature of self-help
there are no empty whiskey bottles,
no cigarettes rolled from fag ends
salvaged from 3 a.m. ashtrays, no fools
in love. There are relaxing bubble baths
and scented candles, of course,
there are people turning cartwheels
in the sand, women in white
boosting their immune system,
drinking Celestial Seasonings Wellness Tea
but no chipped green nail polish,
no one sitting at the dining table
with their boyfriend's daughter,
three bottles of Chardonnay down,
chair-dancing to The Supremes.
There are quests by the dozen,
heart warming tales of triumph
over tragedy but no biting satires,
no comedies of error.
There are angels, spirit guides,
and mystic healers to help you navigate
the path to peace and harmony
but no Eeyore, Scarlet O'Hara
or Don Draper. As for Madam Bovary,
she's signed up for a twelve step programme
with Sex and Love Addicts Anonymous,
where she's sharing how she gets her kicks
from romantic highs, learning that she uses
them as a way to sidestep intimacy.

Smells and bells

If I were to take up religion
I'd want the works –
icons, ceremonial vestments,
a thurible of incense swung
towards the consecrated Eucharist,
the heady smoke of frankincense,
myrrh and copal symbolising
the prayers of saints in heaven.
I'd want a sung liturgy, a choir
singing the Agnus Dei,
Pietàs, altars (not communion tables)
and stained glass windows
depicting the zodiacs
and labours of the months.
Of course, I've only worshipped
at the altar of the self
but you can keep
the mental hygiene of CBT
with its management techniques
and pious smiley-face. I'll take
Jung's messy pantheistic landscapes any day,
the interior peopled by
gods and tricksters, wing-footed
Mercury with his twists and turns,
his fictions and double-dealing,
his whiplash, quicksilver tongue;
Pan, fluting in Arcadia one minute,
inciting panic the next;
morbid, responsible Saturn
trying to teach party-loving
Dionysus a lesson;
and Psyche, naturally, separating

beans from grains in her dark
night of the soul, chained
to the chariot of love while Eros,
born of chaos, shoots himself
with his own arrow.

Fallen angel

Last to go is the halo,
which she carries hooped
like a bag over her arm,
as dented and bruised
as the wheel of a stock car.
The wings went days ago,
along with sweetness of breath
and heart. All she's left with
is an ache between the shoulders,
an occasional urge to take off,
like an amputee preparing
to walk on ghost limbs.
That and a dryness in her mouth,
as if she had swallowed her own feathers.
Today, her feet are blistered from dancing,
her dress and beaded slippers,
the smuts of mascara beneath her eyes,
confess the ruin of last night's revels,
her skin is crusted with salt.
One more song she cried as the band
packed up their instruments,
shimmying to the percussive crash
when the drummer dropped a cymbal.
Later, she rested her head on the shoulder
of a horn player, felt the earth
vibrating through his limbs as he blew,
a sound so soulful, so complete
she wondered how she had ever contemplated
the divine life, all that white,
the cool silver of heavenly ideals.

What do you feel?

As a rule it takes several days,
the mind quarantining
the offending emotion,
a cordon of muscles, nerve endings,
spleen, liver, bowels tensing,
winding tight around the criminal
until your entire body is strung,
your skin as thin as rice paper.
Then your printer jams,
your texts go unanswered
and the cell is ruptured,
the prisoner erupts,
a Vesuvius of nameless, faceless stuff,
all the compacted magma, the volatiles
spitting, ancient history
salting last week's wound.
So when he asks – as they all do –
what do you feel?
you find nothing
in the crater except wings of panic
but because nothing can't be
the right answer you trawl
the recycle bin in your head
and come up with – sad. He likes sad
although you suspect he'd prefer anger,
he'd like you to bawl and shout,
break down
instead of just saying the words
but it's better than nothing and it makes you
feel good, which is the really sad thing.

Instructions for living

Use sparingly.
Keep in a safe place.
Repeat if necessary.
Clean daily to avoid soilage being burnt on.
Avoid prolonged sunlight.
Stand upright in a cool place.
Style as desired.
Do not allow to dry out.
Know your limits.
Wash before use.
Do not use on babies or infants.
Be careful with sharp objects.
Do not use as a toy.
Press play.
Don't rub, as this tends to fluff up the pile.
Do not swallow.
Sit back, relax and enjoy.
Clean the wound and surrounding area.
Repeat.
Dispose of in a dustbin.

Killing mosquitoes with Nabokov's *Lolita*

You can always count
on a fancy prose stylist
for the midnight slaughter
of those whiny bloodsuckers
(paperback, ceiling).

Cat-sitting in Figols

It's the perfect setting for a horror film –
just me, a goatherd, the psychopath next door
and the black cats I'm looking after in this hamlet
high in the Catalan Pyrenees, where there is
no shop, no bar, where even the church doors
haven't creaked open since last September's fiesta.
Plus I have no car, the cooker runs on Calor gas
– cylinders as menacing and hissy as giant wasps –
and the water for the entire village comes from
a tank that threatens to dry up any minute.
Tonight I dragged myself away from the terrace,
from the nightly picture show of shooting stars,
the distant beams of headlights and the twiggy forelegs
of a praying mantis as thin as an extra from *Corpse Bride*,
bracing myself for another sleepless night.
I have slipped a ring on the finger of a fate
that doesn't belong to me. Shackled to a fantasy
that strides further and further away, deep
into the Noguera Pallaresa valley, I argue
with the cartoon version of the self I just can't shrug off,
convinced I'm being watched, sickened by the flies
that arrived in an atomic cloud and settled into a shawl
around my shoulders, mesmerised by the rain-flattened remains
of a dead cat, jaws stretched wide in a silent scream.

What if the mask is all there is?

'Whatever is profound loves masks.' Nietzsche

What if there is no
nugget of naked honesty
at the heart of the onion?
What if peeling
all those layers was no more
than an elaborate game
of pass the parcel, the gift
in each stratum planted
by auto-suggestion, the therapist
an unwitting *agent provocateur*?
What if the private eyes
were looking in the wrong place,
the real clues to be found
in the mask itself –
so that by inhabiting the mask
of a hermit, the one who sits alone
eventually has something
of the cave about her,
her thoughts cowering
in the twilight, her words
smelling of must, her home
a damp basement flat
where mould grows as stealthily
as verdigris on bronze.

Mount Spirit

By the time my spaceship landed
on Mount Spirit I was as empty
as all the other hungry ghosts
holding out begging bowls for a crust
of comfort from someone else's god.

I wanted purified air. I was sick
of myself, my skin as itchy
as a cheap sweater, my anxiety,
hypochondria, all the symptoms
and grandiose failures, the guilt.

All around people were displaying
their wounds, afraid to lick them, scared
they'd be contaminated by their own
anger, jealousy, pride, medicating
those ugly stepchildren with mantras.

But who was it going up the mountain,
whose boots were those outside the door
to the meditation chamber, what I
was whitewashing the mess
of history from my memory banks?

And would I gird my loins for the desert,
fight an epic battle with my heart?
Or would I opt for a relaxing massage,
sweep my disobedient feelings beneath
a non-slip yoga mat at a weekend retreat?

Anywhere but here

After I'd grown out of swishing through the halls
of Hampton Court in a farthingale and ruffs,
skirts of cloth of silver seeded with pearls;
of knocking back Old Fashioneds in Gatsby's world,
dancing till dawn in the gold and lacquer salon
of the Ile de France, the beaded fringe of my back-
                                            less dress
flapping daringly above my knees, I headed
for Montparnasse. I haunted the bistro tables and
                                            couchettes
of Le Select, the covered terrace of Le Dôme
but found no Hemingway or Jean Rhys,
no Kiki dancing, *sans culottes*, at the Jockey.
It was the same in New York; no more Cedar Tavern,
no Pollock to rip the men's room door from its hinges,
no Kerouac to piss in an ashtray. Only Soho
retained the patina of those louche and beautiful
                                            golden ages
where talent and desperado drinking collide.
There, in 1980, you could eat hot salt beef on rye
in a Jewish deli then prop up the bar of the French
beside the fixtures and fittings –
artists on the left, architects on the right,
an emphysemic columnist in a food-stained cravat hissing
at a woman with a cat curled up on her head.
There, it was possible to escape an ordinary life, drink
your Côtes du Rhone and wait for the ghost of Francis
                                            Bacon
to roll in for a glass of champagne *en route* to the Colony.
There, dodge the troublesome question of what I am
so very afraid of discovering right here, right now.

Forgive yourself

Go on, do yourself a favour – forgive yourself. It's essential for a healthy life, according to the weekend Buddhists, it will Dyno-rod your emotional sinuses, tease out the best in you. Imagine it now, that you have forgiven yourself for every major and minor transgression; isn't it kind of wonderful the purity of that Nordic air, filtered by spruce and icy water, as it sluices the once Hogarthian alleyways of your mind, spring-cleans your soul? It's like opening a new notebook, the buttermilk vellum unblemished with weasel words, crossings-out, medallions of spilt ink, the edits and red-inked warnings you can't help making as you go along. Just bathe in the bliss, enjoy the guilt-free ride through the pasteurised present, no looking over the shoulder for the bacterial shadows of the sins – what sins? – of the past. Imagine never again beating yourself up about the hearts you broke, the money you stole from your mother's purse, the unborn child you drowned in a vat of gin, the minor peccadilloes that have you forever muttering Hail Marys to a deaf god. Imagine the slate wiped clean, even remorse, which you are allowed to feel during the first phase of the process, exiled to the hinterlands to chew the fat at the bar of an outlaw saloon alongside guilt, resentment, contrition and blame, each bemoaning their lack of gainful employment. The beauty is there's no statute of limitation on it and no need for repentance either although you have to wonder about the possibility of cheating and the spare time chanters are rather woolly when it comes to the sticky question of self-forgiveness by people like Pol Pot,

Stalin and Peter Sutcliffe, let alone how those with a low IQ might grapple with the Buddhist doctrine of the endlessly ramifying interdependence of everything and the middle road Buddhism takes between free will and determinism. But never mind, we're assuming you're just the average Joe who is being eaten alive by his pain. Because it's a tough old life in the twenty-first century, the soul carbuncled with neglect, the heart clogged from a glut of value-brand choice, great chunks of your mind as pixellated as the face of a clandestine interviewee. Why the hell shouldn't you wake up tomorrow with a clear conscience; after all you've done your yoga, eaten your yoghurt, you damn well deserve your shot of cheap grace.

Beautiful dead things

A bumble bee clinging to the stamens
of a rhododendron, stripes so bleached
it might have overdosed on pollen;
a hessian fly, biscuity wings outstretched
on the bedroom wall, a tiny angel
of the north; ten red roses, petals dried
to the colour of a scab, a bouquet fit
for a corpse bride; and me, a bruised apple
on the bathroom floor, black bib spreading
above the neckline of my green linen dress
as every last drop of blood in my body races
towards my unreachable heart, which went
haywire, then stopped – right after I'd painted
Viva Glam on my now blue lips.

Burn baby burn

Searing my flesh with olive oil
I gave up swotting photosynthesis
to shade the human heart –
purple for aorta and vena cava,
crimson for ventricles and atriums,
those fiery chambers. Naturally,
I failed Biology 'O' level
but what did I care?
All I wanted was to live
forever in a heat wave,
recreate the crucible
of my first summer
when temperatures soared,
'A' line dresses flirted
with tanned knees,
James Dean smouldered
in *Rebel Without a Cause*
and my mother swaddled me
in so many blankets
my skin exploded in a rash,
the doctor said it was a wonder
she hadn't smothered me to death.

Trying to put Lorna together again

It's a job for a team – an osteopath
to straighten my S-bend of a spine,
an acupuncturist to disperse
the damp stagnation in my spleen,
an expert in the Alexander Technique
to teach me how to walk, sit and stand,
an analyst to interpret my dreams
of walled medieval cities, young boys
throwing apples, spontaneous fires
erupting in vast wastelands (I'm reading
a lot of Jung). Each of them gifts me
a different version of myself. Back home
I get out the sticky-back plastic, try to paste
the fragments together but it's all a bit
Heath Robinson and I can no longer tell
whether the Picassoesque quality
of my inner landscape – the heart
where the head should be and vice versa –
is the result of botched reassembly
or an original design flaw.

Tea party for the dead

At the tea party for the dead
the dearly departed are dressed casually,
as if surprised during a game of canasta
or while brushing their teeth. The living,
on the other hand – widowers, orphans, secret lovers –
are suited and booted, buttoned up
against the guilt that at some point they stopped
wailing 'I simply can't go on'.
One day they found themselves looking forward
to a toasted teacake with their morning coffee,
lighting up a Marlboro at the kitchen table,
buying a red dress with a plunging neckline.
Some remain faithful to a memory;
the sheets of others are already stained
with coconut oil. Either way,
a moment often prayed for –
the chance to see their beloved again, release
words that once ached in their throats –
isn't quite what they'd pictured,
what with the sandwiches curling at the edges,
the dead huddled on one side of the room,
the bereaved on the other, both parties
eyeing one another suspiciously,
Montagues and Capulets at a wedding,
each afraid of shattering the images
ambered in the catacombs of their hearts.

Flood

My furniture has walked in the night,
the blue sofa colliding with the white sofa
in a hobnailed pas-de-deux,
the oak chest bloated, belly up, its contents –
a signed copy of *Purple America*; a first edition of *Flush*;
the video I gave my father last Christmas rewound
to his favourite aria; my cat's ashes –
spewed into the toxic sludge on the floor.
Picasso's dreamer slumps in her frame;
streaked with blue tears, a love letter
that will never be rewritten loses
its moment. Outside it's like a war zone,
mounds of broken fridges and sodden chairs,
the stink of damp carpets, festival bogs, despair.
Inside I'm sweeping the same square
of floor, over and over, trying to ignore
a high pitched wail
from the phone that needs its cord cutting,
the screech of messages trapped in purgatory.
Everything is lost.

Flood 2

For a few giddy seconds the prospect of escape
glimmers, that flash of fools' gold. It's my pet fantasy,
the slate wiped clean; no Lot's wife me, I've a knack
for running, not looking back. Three days later,
I'm found gazing into the middle distance,
parcel tape in one hand, book in the other,
surrounded by a dozen half-filled boxes.
Last night the old lady three doors down
tried to kill herself, the burglar who broke into
my house and stole anything worth a cent
from the bone-dry first floor – camera, stereo,
DVD player – left a muddy boot print on my bed
but no fingerprints at the point of exit and entry.

Memorial Day

There is a moment, in the closing seconds
of the final episode of the fifth series
of *The West Wing*, when Martin Sheen,
as President Jed Bartlett, reminds me
of my father. It must be his hair.
It certainly isn't the flashing cameras,
the adulatory roar as Jed steps up to the plate
at Baltimore's Camden Yards.
No crowd ever cheered my dad. Nor is it
Bartlett's anger, fuelled by yet another crisis
in the Middle East although my father
could get riled by foreign affairs, all right,
and he would surely have agreed with
the President when he says he'd like to bomb
the lot of them. But my father's furies
had little impact on the world stage, mostly
his missiles – *you're stupid, nothing, worthless;*
a direct hit from the fist, the flat of his hand –
were aimed at more local targets,
collateral damage rarely incurred beyond
our front door. Although, now I think of it,
the jury's still out on the long term fall-out
of those strikes, the impact reverberating within
the hearts and minds of those primary targets
to this day. So anyway, I think it must be the hair,
a particular way my dad's hair used to look
after he'd run it through with the black comb
he would wet under a tap. Something
intractable about that 1950s wedge, just like
Bartlett's when he raises his arm to bowl
the celebrating pitch on Memorial Day.

Learning to swim

Early morning, low tide, my father holds me
by the waist, ordering me to let my legs float
to the surface. The sea's milky blue, a mobile of gulls
squawks overhead. *You'll let go*, I cry.
He promises to hold fast but my mother's fear –
the magnetic pull of the deep – ripples towards me,
a watery lasso.
          Years later, on a Greek island,
I teach myself to swim – no more paddling
in the shallows, watching as I drift towards the horizon,
wondering when exactly his swollen hands let go.

Fallen tree

For decades I lay here turning bone-like,
so dry I'd have spat and cackled like a witch
on a fire. Then the bark and wood-boring beetles
drilled through my flaking skin, moss and lichens
sprouted, mites burrowed a labyrinth of corridors
where birds, bats and spiders set up home.
Now I'm more magnificent and grounded
than I ever was in my heyday – just look
at these ruffles of bracket fungus, these garlands
of ivy and beads of sulphur tuft. Oh I know
what those cocky saplings are thinking, vaunting
their bendy spines, their lime green leaves.
They see me as a crusty dowager sidelined at a ball,
crammed into the moss velvet she's worn
to every party since Nijinsky choreographed
the *Rite of Spring*. But I don't miss all that jostling
for sunlight and crowing about rookeries, not one bit.
They'll tell you I'm past it but it's all happening in here,
my seedless loins a den, guest house and larder
and maybe, in a century or so, a nursery. See,
the older I get, the more life I have in me.

PART 2

Eclipse

At the eleventh minute of the eleventh hour on the eleventh day of the eighth months of the final year of the millennium, darkness fell. And they left their homes and their places of work to congregate on the beaches and the sea and on the hillsides surrounding the city. And for those two minutes the roads were still and business all along the south coast was suspended, even in advertising they left their Powerpoint pitches to gaze up at the wondrous spectacle. But there was much disappointment throughout the land. Because in the place where there was totality the sky was thick with clouds and in the place where the sun shone there was a partial eclipse, which meant only a very few saw Bailey's beads and the corona and diamond ring, talk of which had excited many before the event. On the beach at Brighton were gathered a multitude with their pinhole cameras and special glasses and they experienced not complete darkness but a strange and eerie light, the like of which they had never known. It was cold. A hush fell over the crowd as the sky darkened. Even the mobile phone ringtones were silent. Even the birds were still and then, as the sun moved from behind the moon, the pigeons and herring gulls burst forth in song, they circled over the Miss Haversham skeleton of the old West Pier and dived through the broken windows of its concert hall. And the crowds left the beach slowly for they had been moved by nature's display and were reluctant to return to their keyboards and faxes, their to-do lists. Even though they had set their videos and knew they would get a better view on TV.

The day Jacko died

It is 10:10 in Seaford (a million miles from New York)
a Friday, eighteen days till Bastille Day, yes
it is 2009 and I eat strawberries
and low-fat Greek yoghurt in the tack-on room I call
the conservatory, I dead-head
the geraniums and count five pea-sized fruits
on the tomato plant in my matchbox of a garden,
I climb the stairs to my office and switch on
the computer and there it is, the news I didn't hear
on the radio because I woke up with an earache,
the wire brush of neuralgia prickling my scalp
from the inside, a spaced-out feeling that makes life
move in slow motion and when I get that feeling
I listen to Radio 3 because I can't stand the news,
all that jabber, the politicians brilliantining their way
past the sharpened teeth of terrier journos.
Waiting for emails to drop into my inbox I go
to the window to check on the trio of seagull chicks
on my neighbour's roof. One of them is dead.
It's lying face down wings bent awkwardly either side,
body swarming in flies. It's only a bird,
for god's sake, but I've been looking out for these chicks
since they hatched and I'm sobbing my heart out.
I don't cry for Michael. Oh, I'm sad, like we're all sad
and I'm a media rubber-necker all day, craning
my sternothyroids to get the latest on the missing doctor,
the tributes, the mystery of his final 24 hours, 'cause this is
chilling, thrilling and it's all mixed up, somehow,
the flattened body of the dead chick,
Jacko's lost childhood, his silent-movie-star mask,
and I am having palpitations by now and thinking of
how I collapsed on the bathroom floor another hot

day, how I was the same age as Jackson, that whisper
of a man, when my heart twitched
to a halt temporarily and I stopped breathing.

Crime of the century

Burning up inside, Ethel Rosenberg gets dressed
as if she's going to a gala. For one bright moment
everything forgotten: her brother's lies, evidence –
typewriter, console table, notes burning in a frying pan –
as flimsy as her nylons. She remembers only Julie's touch,
his pencilled love letters, the arias she sung him
from an adjoining cell. And then he's there, her husband,
and the room has no screen and they charge and grasp,
mouths, hands, flesh. Prised apart by guards. Julie's face
so smeared with lipstick he looks as if he's bleeding.

That last hot evening, their fourteenth anniversary,
they finger kiss through wire mesh, blood trickling
down the screen. At 8.06, just before the setting sun
heralds the Jewish Sabbath over Sing-Sing, Julius is dead.
Minutes later, Ethel, in a green print dress, settles
tight lips into a Mona Lisa smile. Says nothing,
winces as the electrode cap makes contact with her skull.
It takes five shocks to kill her, the oak chair made
for a man, Ethel so petite the helmet doesn't fit, so fried
witnesses see coils of smoke rising from her head.

She dreamed of being an opera singer but who was she
to have such dreams, product of the Jewish Bronx,
a mother who belittled her, said she brought it on herself?
Anyway, her mouth would never open wide enough,
except to kiss him, her beloved Julius. His crime?
Handing over minor secrets. Hers was finding love
one New Year's Eve, just before she went onstage to sing.
He cooled her flaming nerves. Never having known such caring
she hurled herself into her role – loyal wife, so insignificant
to the KGB, she didn't even have a code name.

La Divina

'First I lost weight, then I lost my voice, now I've lost Onassis.'

I

It had to be witchery, tapeworms or amphetamines, they said,
how else could that fat, frumpy Greek with her bad skin
and frizzy hair, her elephant's legs, that peasant in her
                                                    Sunday best
transform herself into a goddess in Yves St Laurent, a Nefertiti
with sculpted hair and eyebrows, those iconic sweeps of kohl?
Try two years of being hungry, dear, try sheer hard work
and willpower. Try shedding everything in the service of
                                                    your art.
You think singing Brünnhilde and Elvira in one season
was a *folie de grandeur*? La Divina will be tougher still,
                                                    demanding
painstaking attention, that you carry yourself like a statue.

II

Hard work, yes, but the girl born with nothing but a voice
is used to that. Because even the voice is flawed: ugly, heavy,
sometimes shrill, sometimes hollow and you work, work,
                                                    work
until you can change its timbre, colour and weight at will.
How they fete you then, sixteen encores after your debut at the
                                                    Met!
But the bouquets soon sprout thorns – snapped snarling
                                                    backstage
you're a tigress who needs to be tamed; too ill to sing in Rome
you're a prima donna. Sharpening their pencils, the hacks
hone the myth of your tantrums and walkouts and you
discover goddesses are not allowed a moment's weakness,

51

especially the mortal weakness of love, which is the wrong kind
of sacrifice. And to stoop so low for it, to gild that Greek satyr,
sip champagne on barstools upholstered in the foreskins of
whales.

Now you're fallen, frivolous, a scarlet woman prey to human
passions like the rest of us, only more so because you're just too
large and in life as in art, you give and demand everything.
Too bad

you fall for a man whose understanding of women comes from
a Van Cleef & Arpels catalogue, who'll shoo you off the Christina
to clear the decks and snare his next trophy while you hole up
in Paris, fade away listening to the voice of La Callas in her
heyday.

Moments of being

What a plunge!
Water, the most feminine of elements,
its silky embrace, icy heart,
its undercurrents, fogs and dews.
Water, created when stars are born.
A burst of sunlight dapples the surface
of the Ouse, reminding her
of a child's bedroom in St. Ives,
the waves
breaking on the beach,
the little acorn of the blind
drawn back and forth across the floor.
That was ecstasy, that
was life.

Pearl

We picture you in the Chelsea Hotel
limousines purring outside,
the ice-cream sheen of Leonard's cum
pearling your quivering lips. Or onstage,
white blues mama, shimmering in silver lamé,
mouth wide in the ecstatic throes of joy or pain –
who the hell knows, man? Ripping out
each note, ripping out heart, lungs, throat,
that unholy howl unpacking the smokestacks
of Port Arthur, its cheerleader ideal, the prom
no one invited you to, ugly duckling,
the irritant lodged in your heart, which you choked
with beads and feathers, speed and horse,
Southern Comfort, that wild cackle laugh.
You were the hottest chick in town, could out-ball
any guy but no man made you feel as good
as an audience and if pearls are tears of the gods
yours were shed in private, that wisecracking shell
hiding the square dream of love and picket fences
you never quite left behind on Pearl's road to fame.
The day you bought it at the Landmark Motel,
face down, wedged between wall and bed
in panties and blouse, your lip cut, fisting a handful
of silver and bills, your life zapped
by the too-pure heroin you skin-popped earlier,
you'd called City Hall about a marriage license,
never dreaming your fiancé would be removing his pants
in a game of strip billiards at the moment you'd lay
your works in a Chinese box and lurch forwards.

Missing

All night she waits for him, praying
for the sound of his footsteps, dreading it,
and when she hears him stumbling
up the steep staircase, her stomach knots
and then he crashes into the studio
babbling about a boat that is coming
to take him to a miraculous country.
Don't touch me, she thinks as he lurches
towards her. *Touch me*, she pleads
after he has blacked out. She loosens
his red neckerchief, discerns a new smell
mingling with the reek of alcohol seeping
from his open mouth, his pores.

*

What to make of her? That dreamy gaze,
those almond eyes, her swan's neck
and alabaster skin. Modigliani
has been painting this woman all his life;
before he clapped eyes on her
she was his ideal woman. Unlike
Beatrice Hastings, who matched the man
she called her pale and ravishing villain
absinthe for absinthe, rage for rage,
Jeanne is impossible to pin down.
One day he's seen dragging her by the hair,
incensed by the way she disappears
into the slipstream of his shadow.

*

Sewing a life out of love and art
she makes her own clothes and jewellery,
wears a damask turban threaded with gold,
a woollen cape, gypsy boots. She paints herself
at an easel, vulpine, determined, looking furtively
over her shoulder. However neatly she stitches,
the seam that is Amadeo keeps unravelling.

*

The sardines stain the sheets.
Jeanne feeds Modi straight from the can
spooning silvery forkfuls into his parched mouth.
For a moment the smell of the fish masks
the stench of their unwashed bodies,
reminds her of their time in Nice and how,
back home, he painted the walls
ochre and orange, the colours of heat.
She chews grey flesh, bites into soft bones –
she could devour all of him like this.

*

In a lucid interval he binds their wrists
with gold packing cord. Later, she picks her way
across the carpet of charcoal, coal and matches
to sit at the table and sketch their wedded hands.

*

There is no heat, no water; Jeanne wets
her lover's lips with a rag soaked in rum,
the drink he took against his cough, spits
into his mouth. She'd give him her own blood
if she could but there are times she has to bite
into her fisted knuckles, afraid she might
strangle him for dousing his TB like a martyr.

*

On the seventh day Ortiz finds her clinging
to Modi's lifeless body, the windows blank
with frost, the bed strewn with bottles.

*

3 a.m. Jeanne Hébuterne opens the window
of her childhood bedroom, turns to face
her fashion sketches tacked to the wall,
her ghostly image in a full length mirror.
She is 21 years old, nine months pregnant,
five floors up. She steps out backwards, vainly
hoping, perhaps, to save her unborn child.

Tomorrow never knows

'You see, there's something else I'm going to do, something I must do –
only I don't know what it is... All I know is, this isn't it for me.'
                                        JOHN LENNON, March 1966

Famous and loaded, hotter than Jesus, the smart, gobby one
takes a breather from being a Beatle, from the secure schedule
of interviews and recording, tours that are a cross
between the new testament and *Satyricon*, the multitudes
clutching at their hems, convinced the saviours
from Liverpool can make the lame walk, the blind see, help
the averagely confused see the light, while backstage
the emperors are having a ball, hotel rooms
a bacchanal of booze, drugs, groupies and whores.
John's always known he was a genius but even so it's
                                                  fantastic!
This boy from the sticks taking over the world.
It's also a honey trap. Still, he'd be a fool
to give it up and no one with a ticket for the gravy train,
none of the fucking peasants who don't know anything,
can't feel anything without the fab four doing it first
wants Rome to burn before the bubble bursts.
But the rags to riches romance is on the turn; adrift
in the stockbroker belt of Surrey, John stuffs
his palatially carpeted halfway house
with the passing fads and fancies he buys almost daily
at Asprey's – phones and gadgets that don't work, a gorilla
                                                  suit,
a compendium of games in a box he can't close – restlessly
seeking the answer to a question he can't frame,
hiding a pain too big to feel behind a quip, a barb,
those self-conscious grins. Hell-bent on torching his ego
– Christ, what's he got to lose? –
he knocks back LSD like it's candy, switches off his mind

and floats downstream on a rain of endless words,
the best he's ever written, and it's this nowhere man,
this millionaire shadow who washes up at the Indica gallery
one November evening, hoping to find an orgy.
Instead he's handed a card telling him to breathe.
He gulps air like a newborn, sucking the black and white
newsreels of Beatlemania into a vortex.
It's as if his entire life has been gunning towards this moment,
this meeting, this bite of the apple, the make-believe nail
he drives home with an imaginary hammer,
sparking the tinder of his bark-dry soul,
laying the foundations of his next incarceration.

My Billie Holiday years

Singing along to Billie's records in my sitting room,
Budwar bottle for a mic, I picture myself sheathed
in a silver dress as clingy as the scales of a fish.
The way she sings *lover man oh where can you be?*
in that bluesy, tattered voice of hers
she could have ripped it right from my own soul.
In another room, egged on by my therapist,
I'm elevating my childhood to operatic heights
of dysfunction, multiplying the burns
on my ashtray of a heart. It's not your
common or garden unhappy upbringing I'm after;
no, I aspire to a marriage of glamour and tragedy –
Billie's heart-wrung vocals hypnotising men in suits
and hourglass women who sip Sidecars and Pink Ladies
at the lamp-lit tables of The Coconut Grove.
It's perfectly captured in that photograph of Billie
in satin jacket, diamante necklace and earrings,
a pair of Chihuahuas cradled in her arms. She's leaning in
to get a light for the cigarette clamped between her lips
from her Mafiosi husband. They're both focused intently
on the flame of the match and I imagine her drawing hard
on the cigarette, exhaling in an *I don't take any bullshit*
kind of way. Only she did, of course, and looking back
from another couch I want to disown that young woman
singing to her futon as if her heart would break
from all the troubles she's had, worried that even
her cool is only skin deep, that *I don't give a shit* shrug
nothing more than an echo of the smile she fixed
to her face all those years ago, a look so detached
from her heart it's taken on a life of its own.

Escape artist

As you slipped
through the gap
between window and sill
your face momentarily
eclipsed
by a fog of icy breath
did you imagine
you might materialise
there in the luminal night
or were you hoping
to take flight
on torn paper wings,
enigmatic angel
of Rome, Providence Island,
the Lower East Side?
What disordered geometry
lured you to the window
in the first place,
what Euclidean elements
angled your body as you
emerged or vanished
behind wallpaper,
the crumbling stucco
of a derelict loft,
flattened yourself
against a wall, behind glass;
what interior fugue played
while you veiled your face,
slowing the exposure
of your Yashica Reflex?
Slithery as an eel, you
and your ghostly body

of work slip right through
the theories, leaving
only the trail of prints
that may, or may not,
be suicide notes.

PART 3

Please may I not have a man

Please may I not have a man who grates
banana over muesli for breakfast; who wears corduroy trousers,
a blazer with gold cuff buttons, tee shirts with slogans
or one of those stupid woolly hats with ear flaps;
who drinks elderflower cordial and decaffeinated tea;
who gossips or chatters like a girl;
who can't get an erection and doesn't bother
to score any Viagra; who sleeps with another woman –
another poet come to that – because he needs to prove
he's still got what it takes; who harps on about the glory
of his student days, twenty five years on;
who will promise you the earth and deliver
a pepperoni pizza from Tesco, reduced to £1.39;
who is in therapy. Especially don't give me a man
who is in therapy, who would rather chew over his issues
than crack open a bottle of wine, who will try to analyse
my dreams and clog up my inbox with his cod
psychology and Hallmark sentiments, emailing me,
for instance, about his struggle to scale my ivory tower.
No, I want a man who doesn't have much to say
about himself; who stalks the Downs like a Nordic god
with his dog; who loves steak pies and bangers and mash;
rinses my hair with jugs of water in the bath;
who drops by with a bacon sandwich when I'm hung-over;
who is bringing me back to life
with keepsakes of his world – lamb's tail, crow's feather,
sea-kale, lichen-encrusted bark – and teaching me to love
January, without counting down the days to July.

Penguin

It's made of velvet, black body,
mushroom chest, yellow collar and
skew-whiff bow tie, a red beak that looks
as if it smashed, cartoon-style, into a door
one drunken night. Fifties you reckon
although it reminds me of the jazz age,
beaded cocktails and flapper dresses,
Gatsby's garden lit up like a Christmas tree,
a sad little waltz at the end of the evening,
a lone figure weaving across the lawn,
spilling champagne in his wake.
The wing I flapped in farewell the night
you gave me the penguin leans raffishly
on a speaker, reminder of those exquisite,
excruciating Sunday roasts in the days
when a green light was too much to hope for
and, after you'd slipped the lipstick kiss
I'd left on a napkin into your wallet,
you'd drive me home in nerve-wracked, thrilling
silence, our tongues, hands and hearts tied.

Voltage

Positioning a postcard on the *Letters of Ted Hughes*
you show me which side of the bed you sleep on,
and where your dog sleeps. I do the same,
for me and my cat, and it's clear we've each been
keeping a place free – you on the right, facing left,
the empty space in front of you; me on the left,
filling it in. It's almost as if we could slot into
one another's lives and barely disturb the sheets
although from the charge in my kitchen as you check
the socket that keeps blowing my fairy lights
I imagine there might be quite a bit of sheet ruffling
when the time comes to strip off your checked shirt
and black jeans, my skin tight grape sweater,
beneath which my bosoms are squealing
and giggling with all the subtlety of a tavern wench.

Purring like Gina Lollobrigida

Since the night of a thousand kisses,
those kisses with a language
all their own, a language that is – dare
I say it? – like a film score in its sweep,
now orchestrated by an invisible hand
that lingers over every quaver and semi-quaver,
glides effortlessly from *andante* to *agitato*;
now plunging into anarchy as the string section
breaks loose, playing with a violence that snaps
every *Pirastro Passione*. It's the kissing of explorers,
the kissing of the explored. It's kissing
that bruises the lips, shreds the skin.
Anyway, since then I've felt like a star,
striding like Bette Davis, purring
like Gina Lollobrigida, pouting
like Brigitte Bardot. In the bath
this morning, I sponged foam from my legs
and it was every bit as Hollywood
as the unexpected snow that's falling now,
another little miracle, heaven sent.

I could drink a case of you

I'm pouring a glass of Chablis
when I notice it, the scent
of our afternoon pleasure
on my hand, the smell of you,
and it's a perfect coming together –
your mineral, fermented bouquet
and the chilled teardrop
sliding down the glass,
like the blending of musty delight
with the tart aftertaste of melancholy
that bites the back of my throat
whenever we part.

Why do you drink so much?

Because it's in my blood, my first home
a pub – the fug of smoke, the casky smell of ale,
the rainbow gleam of optics as nourishing
as a mother's milk to me. Because I like it,
the straw and citrus pith of Chablis,
the vanilla and spice of Rioja,
the duet of cucumber and rose petal
in Hendrick's gin. I love the celebratory pop
of a cork, the Mad Men rattle of ice in a glass,
the convivial hum of a Friday night bar.
I like the rituals and accoutrements –
cocktail shaker, hand-blown glasses, waiter's corkscrew.
I like imbibers a whole lot more than abstainers
and although the honeymoon is over, despite
the disappointments, disagreements, trial separations –
drinking and me, we're in it for the long haul
and on the whole I prefer the looser, well-oiled me,
the garrulous, embarrassing one to the parched one
counting units in the corner, spoiling every drink.

Mixing the perfect Martini

Allow a shaft of sun to shine through
a bottle of vermouth until it strikes
the Bombay Sapphire you've poured
into a jug frosted with ice. You're aiming
to simulate the immaculate conception,
the Holy Ghost piercing the Virgin's hymen,
in the words of St Thomas Aquinas,
'like a ray of sunlight through a window –
leaving it unbroken'. Never shake,
you'll bruise the gin and chip the ice,
turn out the most unholy of cocktails
– a weak and bitter Martini. Stir,
and the molecules will lie sensuously one
on top of the other, bringing to mind
Dorothy Parker's need to stop at three
- in case she ended up under her host.
Use only Noilly Prat, the aromatic wine
infused with a secret blend of herbs
and spices, aged in casks outside
to replicate ancient sea voyages.
Drink only with the most charming
and erudite of companions –
David Niven, Noel Coward and Mae West
spring to mind – never alone unless
you're Jack London and live in a hideaway
called Wolf House in the Valley of the Moon,
in which case no one will argue when you ask
your local bartender to mix vast quantities
and ship them up to you each night.

More fun than Nigella

in your kitchen the Sunday you burned
the eggs. You tasted of coffee, bacon,
my future. We were whipping up a storm
all that lip smacking and finger licking,
a searing heat as we jammed ourselves
against the fridge, tossing jeans, shirts, underwear
on to the wine rack. You basted
my breasts with coconut oil, I kneaded
and rolled you between sticky palms.
Breathless, panting, our desire
marinating all week, the wanting
so urgent I could have torn your flesh
from your bones with my teeth,
I could have swallowed you whole,
I couldn't get enough of you, our savage hunger
cocktailed with a soupcon of sorrow,
the angel's breath evaporating as we folded
into one another, your chin shredding mine
but I didn't care, I didn't care about anything
but that smouldering moment, the fire alarm
could have blared its warning
and it wouldn't have stopped me
from having to have you, from being had
up against the butcher's block,
the butler's sink, the stove.

I could eat a house

Starting with the raspberry rug
on the bedroom floor,
the taste of cat's paws and dead shrews,
I'd move on to the bed –
love, sweat, the skin we shed each night –
and then to the study
where I'd devour every word,
chewing through books, phrases caged
in my computer and those half-formed ones
hanging like cigarette smoke
just below the ceiling. I'd gnaw my way
through stairs, banisters, the pine chest
in the hall and then I'd get started
on the sitting room. I'd suck
the candy-coloured Riihimäki glass
slowly, saving the orange ones till last,
and move into the kitchen, every surface
– dresser, tea plates, chequered oilcloth –
seasoned as an old frying pan
from our devotional offerings: toad,
roast chicken, baked sea bream
with lemon and anchovy potatoes.
I'd make sure all the lamps were lit
before swallowing them, so the winter
of my interior might be as welcoming
as a lone house on a moor, lights blazing
on a cold December afternoon.
Last of all I'd eat the front door,
complete with brass fox knocker,
so I could always hear you knocking
and be sure to have a way to let you in.

X

after Robert Frost

The way she texted him
a single kiss
the cross flaunting itself
on the screen

to no end
has pierced my heart
and soured some part
of a day I had savoured.

When they opened up my heart

they found a star-struck schoolgirl singing
show tunes down the aisles of morning assembly,

an entire *corps de ballet*, tiny dancers pencilled in
the margins of my unfinished maths homework,

a land rover, a safari hat, the fading paw prints
of the lioness I was born to rear and set free,

a picket fence, dismantled and dusty, stacked
alongside an empty crib, as good as new,

a blue stocking, wrapped around a pack of cheroots
and a dog-eared copy of *The Brothers Karamazov*

and you, waving from your stable door, future perfect
in checked shirt and black scarf, spiv shoes.

Sunday matinée

I

Jiggling a bag of chocolate peanuts and raisins
like a purse of pearls in my palm I dreamed of a life
where women in oyster satin ate men in suits and hats
alive, delivered electric one-liners over bone-dry martinis.
They never smudged their lipstick. I never dreamed
of a *Saturday Night, Sunday Morning* kind of life, didn't picture
myself lying on tarry pebbles beneath the Palace Pier,
a boy's hand up my angora sweater, cold, twiddling my nipples
as if searching for Radio Caroline, my hand in his jeans,
gripping his trapped animal warmth. Tossing him off
I'm somewhere else, on the deck of an ocean liner, windswept,
gazing into the eyes of a mysterious stranger as he lights
two cigarettes, hands one of them – and the stars – to me.

II

After making love on the red and black acreage of your bed
we settle back to watch *Atonement* and drink Chilean wine.
I've seen it before, I've read the book, so in theory I'm prepared
for the postmodern ending, the authorial sleight of hand
that snatches away the happy ever after but just this once
I'd like the film to end at Cuckmere Haven, where we walked
earlier.
I'd like the lovers to live forever in the coastguard cottage
we call Our Dream Home. In this version they don't die,
they don't even get old or fall out of love, they're down there still
laughing on the beach, threatened only by the waves.

Nuzzle

Remember the horses nuzzling in a field,
head to tail, the muzzle of each rubbing

the haunch of the other, the holy stillness
that penetrated the air around them,

how we felt as if we'd stumbled
across a scene too intimate to witness?

That's how it is to wake in your arms, your hands
cupping my breasts, stroking my belly

your hardness pressing against me. I want
to turn to face you but I'm afraid I'll burst

the membrane of this dream, afraid I'll surface
in a shock of bubbles and gulped air –

a young girl's fear of swimming out of her depth,
of the hooves gathering pace beneath her.

Knit me a love song

Waking with my face pressed
into your chest, your arms wrapped
around me, my left leg locked
between your thighs I am
a knitting needle jammed
into a ball of wool.
Not one of those grey, spindly ones
but a chunky rosewood number
(I've been sunbathing),
the wool olive green, the kind
you'd make a loose-knit
sweater out of, the sort
a rock star farmer might wear
with striped drainpipe jeans
and suede shoes, long and pointy
enough to crochet
a stubbled kiss from the earth.

Love dad

You sign the card we're sending your daughter
to wish her luck in her new flat, *love dad xxx*.

Beside that 'dad' my scribbled name appears slight
and I find myself imagining the unimaginable,

damning the shy maternal itch I wrote off with such
a flourish, the ink that will fade away, leaving no trace.

Love is also

the itch
of ancient wounds:
the cries of unborn babies,
homes we can never return to,
a family heirloom of silence,
the sweet torture of breathing
from another room,
the horror of an overnight bag
packed with the clothes
of a stranger.

Winter mornings

Pulling on the knickers you left to warm
on the radiator while you go for a Sunday paper
I am taken back to winter mornings as a child,
exhaling clouds of condensed breath
in my fridge of a bedroom, reaching out
to trace a finger across a kingdom of frost
on the window pane, inhaling the blue smell
of paraffin from the hall. Freeing myself
from a straitjacket of blankets,
my winceyette pyjama warmth evaporates
as I wiggle chilblained feet into red slippers
with rainbow pom-poms and rush downstairs
to the kitchen where the dog is having
a phantom pregnancy, guarding a plastic elephant
with her life, and a doughy gust blooms
from the oven, the door left open
by my mother to warm the school shirt draped
over the back of a chair. It's the embrace
of the cotton I remember as I slide on my knickers,
the little pleasures of those mornings: a favourite song
played on Radio 1, the days she saved me
the creamy top of the milk for my Cornflakes,
a rare favour doled out in her realm
of squirreled apples, buttoned lips, bottled love.

Don't still, my beating heart

We're born with a finite number of heartbeats,
according to the ancient yogis, who counselled calm,
the steering clear of things that make our heart rate
quicken, bring us closer to death. But who wants
to be prudent when it comes to the heart?
I'd rather splurge, fritter my remaining heartbeats
on grape suede shoes and a plum crêpe dress,
slide on stockings you'll later peel off
(there goes a few days' worth), gamble them
drinking Rioja and Hendrick's gin by the fire,
dancing to Goran Bregović on Spotify,
eating your perfect roasties, crumbed with lemon
and thyme (crisp as autumn outside, fluffy
as pillows inside). Talking of pillows, I'd like
to spend more time in your bed, your hips clamped
between my thighs, or drifting into sleep, face to face,
foreheads touching, arms and legs entwined.

Living life to the full

Even for those of us given a second chance
life isn't all cupcakes and drinking iced Earl Grey
laced with gin from bone china teacups,
you can't eat pheasant cooked in apples and cider
every night, can't always wash it down with Mersault,
the colour of polished bronze.
Neither can you continually gasp at the beauty
of things – the womanly curves of the Seven Sisters,
the knit one, purl one of waves slipping over
the needle of the groin at Splash Point. Sometimes
it's a murder of crows circling a confused fox.
It's sliding into the bathwater your lover has just
stepped out of, it's bubble and squeak,
a bottle of cheap red, a slice of peanut butter on toast
while vegging out to *Come Dine With Me*,
suppressing a scream when you can't find any tarragon
in Sainsbury's, hoping the cat kills the mouse it brings home
rather than leaving it half-dead and panting on the patio,
flies feasting on its skinned back. As for dancing
as if no-one's watching, even when I'm on my own
I like to imagine an audience, captivated
by my shimmies, my Cuban hip action, how I manage
to be wild and self-contained all at the same time.

Notes

p. 19 'Live in the moment'
Described as 'paying attention in a particular way: on purpose, in the present moment, and non-judgmentally', mindfulness practice, inherited from the Buddhist tradition, is increasingly used in Western psychology to alleviate a variety of mental and physical conditions – often in combination with cognitive behavioural therapy (CBT).

But how aware are we of the present moment? Studying how the brain produces conscious awareness, Benjamin Libet discovered that we unconsciously decide to act or respond to an event well before we think we've made the decision to act. The time delay between neural events and experience is half a second, which suggests that mental processes can be completed before we have any awareness – that when we think we become conscious of a moment of experience the mind has already started going about its business of evaluating, labelling and judging.

p. 21 'Little pricks'
Qi is a concept in Chinese philosophy and medicine, roughly translated it means the vital energy thought to be inherent in all things. Most acupuncture points are said to exist on meridians or channels through which blood and qi flow.

p. 24 'Smells and bells'
CBT works on the premise that moods and emotions are influenced by patterns of thinking. It teaches people skills to change behaviour and beliefs in order to get rid of or manage problematic symptoms, such as anxiety, depression and shyness, where traditional

psychotherapy sees them as clues to an inner truth.

p. 55 'Missing'
Biographical information about Jeanne Hebuterne is scarce and often ambiguous. Jeanne was Amadeus Modigliani's last lover and muse, and an artist in her own right. She was nine months pregnant when Modigliani, penniless and destitute, died of tubercular meningitis on 24 January, 1920. The following day, Jeanne walked backwards out a fifth floor window in her parental home, killing herself and the unborn child. Originally interred in the Cimetière de Bagneaux, her family, who blamed Modigliani for her death, relented ten years later and her remains were moved to rest beside Modi in Père Lachaise Cemetery. His epitaph reads: "Struck down by Death at the moment of glory." Hers reads: "Devoted companion to the extreme sacrifice."

p. 58 'Tomorrow never knows'
is the final track on *Revolver*, released in 1966, a pivotal year for the band, and in particular John Lennon who met Yoko Ono at the Indica Gallery, where she was holding an exhibition. The humour in Ono's work appealed to John's sense of the absurd. In one piece, 'Hammer and Nail', patrons hammered a nail into a wooden board, creating the art piece. Although the exhibition hadn't opened, Lennon wanted to hammer a nail into the clean board but Ono stopped him. Gallery owner John Dunbar asked her, "Don't you know who this is? He's a millionaire! He might buy it." Ono apparently hadn't heard of the Beatles, but relented on condition that Lennon

paid her five shillings. Lennon replied, "I'll give you an imaginary five shillings and hammer an imaginary nail in." He later said, "That's when we really met. That's when we locked eyes, and she got it and I got it, and that was it."

p. 61 'Escape artist'
Francesca Woodman started taking photographs in 1972, when she was thirteen. Most of her photographs feature herself; many of the images are blurred by camera movement and slow exposure times while others depict her apparently fading into a flat plane, merging with walls or dissolving into the floor. In January 1981 she published an artist's book, *Some Disordered Interior Geometries*, consisting of small photographs and fragments of diary entries pasted over an introduction to Euclid in a nineteenth-century school exercise book she bought in Rome. The same month she jumped out of the window of her Lower East Side loft.

p. 68 'Purring like Gina Lollobrigida'
Pirastro Passione is a make of violin string.

Biographical note

LORNA THORPE was born in Brighton where she lived for most of her life until relocating to Cornwall in 2011. Before turning her hand to poetry she worked as a tour operator, social worker and barmaid. Her debut publication *Dancing to Motown* (Pighog Press, 2005) was a Poetry Book Society pamphlet choice, and her first full collection *A Ghost in My House* was published in 2008.

As a fiction writer, her short stories have been short-listed for awards, and appeared in magazines and anthologies. She works as a freelance writer and has published features in the *Guardian*.

Selected titles in Arc Publications'
POETRY FROM THE UK / IRELAND,
include:

LIZ ALMOND
The Shut Drawer
Yelp!

D M BLACK
Claiming Kindred

JAMES BYRNE
Blood / Sugar

JONATHAN ASSER
Outside The All Stars

DONALD ATKINSON
In Waterlight: Poems New,
Selected & Revised

ELIZABETH BARRETT
A Dart of Green & Blue

JOANNA BOULTER
Twenty Four Preludes & Fugues on
Dmitri Shostakovich

THOMAS A CLARK
The Path to the Sea

TONY CURTIS
What Darkness Covers
The Well in the Rain
folk

JULIA DARLING
Sudden Collapses in Public Places
Apology for Absence

CHRIS EMERY
Radio Nostalgia

LINDA FRANCE
You are Her

KATHERINE GALLAGHER
Circus-Apprentice
Carnival Edge

CHRISSIE GITTINS
Armature

RICHARD GWYN
Sad Giraffe Café

MICHAEL HASLAM
The Music Laid Her Songs in Language
A Sinner Saved by Grace
A Cure for Woodness

GLYN HUGHES
A Year in the Bull-box

MICHAEL HULSE
The Secret History

CHRISTOPHER JAMES
Farewell to the Earth

BRIAN JOHNSTONE
The Book of Belongings

JOEL LANE
Trouble in the Heartland
The Autumn Myth

HERBERT LOMAS
The Vale of Todmorden
A Casual Knack of Living
(COLLECTED POEMS)

PETE MORGAN
August Light

MICHAEL O'NEILL
Wheel

MARY O'DONNELL
The Ark Builders

IAN POPLE
An Occasional Lean-to
Saving Spaces

PAUL STUBBS
The Icon Maker

LORNA THORPE
A Ghost in My House

MICHELENE WANDOR
Musica Transalpina
Music of the Prophets

JACKIE WILLS
Fever Tree
Commandments